SPRING PROGRAMS
for the CHURCH
No. 1

Compiled by
Judith Ann Sparks

Cover Photo
© 1977 by Robert Cushman Hayes
All Rights Reserved

STANDARD PUBLISHING
Cincinnati, Ohio   8731

ISBN: 0-87239-253-8
© 1979, The STANDARD PUBLISHING Co., Cincinnati, Ohio
division of STANDEX INTERNATIONAL Corp.
Printed in U.S.A.

CONTENTS

EASTER

The Man

(A Monologue)

Suzanne Holt

What am I doing here? I've got to leave this place . . . How many times have I said that? . . . It must have been a hundred. It seems like days have passed . . . since the first time I saw THIS MAN.

It was really only hours ago . . .

I was standing out in the crowd. He was up in the palace with Pilate the governor. He was being tried for . . . refusing to pay taxes? And for claiming to be a king. Anyway, that's what the woman standing beside me said.

I wish I could have heard what was going on inside the palace. Pilate kept coming out—he was pretty shook-up. I never saw a man THAT tense, THAT rattled, THAT scared. His eyes were wide open, but He wasn't really looking at anything. His hands were clenched tight—except every now and then he'd squeeze one and then the other, or pound his fist against his palm. His expression was serious . . . no . . . not serious . . . desperate! He swallowed a lot, and he breathed deeply . . . like every breath might be his last.

Just before saying anything, he scanned the crowd, looking for someone who obviously wasn't there.

"I find no fault in him! None at all!"

The people were silent.

"You have a custom—that I should release one prisoner at the Passover. Do you want me to release the King of the Jews?"

"NO! NO!" Everybody was yelling . . . "NOT HIM! But Barabbas!"

One of the chief contributors looked at me as if to say,

"Why aren't *you* involved?" I tried to join them. "Give us Barabbas (weakly)." That's all I could manage. I glanced over at the man who was glancing over at me. "I'm just getting over laryngitis." Actually I just COULDN'T say it any louder.

The noise died down a little . . . Pilate hesitated, then went back into the palace. I wondered what was going on in his mind . . . and in his palace, too.

Pretty soon he was out again, trying to reason with an unreasonable mob. "Look, I'm bringing him out to you so that you'll know—I find no fault in him."

And then Jesus came out wearing an elegant royal robe— dark, deep purple—and a crown . . . of thorns. I squinted. Drops of blood formed a lining for that crown. I got a sick feeling inside as I saw fresh beads of red push the old ones away . . . the old ones flowed into his eyes and across his face like little streams.

Pilate looked at him . . . then at the crowd.

"Here is the man," he said.

THE MAN—

And there he was—the man.

The crowd shouted. "Crucify him! CRUCIFY HIM!" I looked down at the ground and watched an ant trying to carry a large stick. Pilate told them, "YOU take him, and YOU crucify him."

Some of the Jewish leaders spoke up: "We have a law, and according to that law he must die, because he claimed to be the Son of God."

At those words, an expression like I'd never observed before came over Pilate's face. Fear . . . questions . . . anxiousness invaded his eyes, like a child who has just come upon a terrible surprise. He asked Jesus, "Where did you come from?"

But Jesus didn't answer; he didn't move. He was just . . . strangely peaceful.

"DO YOU REFUSE TO SPEAK TO ME? DON'T YOU REALIZE I HAVE POWER TO FREE YOU OR TO CRUCIFY YOU?"

Then Jesus *did* answer him . . . and the answer nearly knocked Pilate off his feet. "You have no power over me that was not given to you from above."

And . . . the way he said it, if you hadn't known that he was

6

just a man, you might have believed it!

Pilate tried again to plead with us, but the Jews just kept yelling, "If you let this man go, you're no friend of Caesar's. Anyone who claims to be a king is Caesar's enemy!"

"Then, HERE is YOUR KING," was Pilate's reply.

The crowd didn't like that, and they began to act wild and senseless. "TAKE HIM AWAY! CRUCIFY HIM!"

"Shall I crucify YOUR KING?"

The chief priests assured him, "We have no king but Caesar." And then Pilate gave in . . . He handed him over to be killed.

The soldiers shoved him around a little while, and made a few disgusting comments before they got him moving up the road. With his bruised arms and hands, he carried his own cross. It was laid across his bleeding back and shoulders, nearly raw from beatings and scourgings earlier that day.

As he went, I could see the strain on his face. He gazed ahead intently toward the hill of Golgotha, where he was to be executed. There was determination in his eyes. It wasn't like the soldiers were leading him, but like he was leading them.

All the while, the pain was so evident! He would flinch when the rugged wood grazed a fresh wound; he would stagger slightly under the load of the cross every now and then. His body would tense as ignorant onlookers threw dirt and rubble into those deep red furrows left by the scourging. I think, though, it probably hurt him just as badly when mothers and fathers sent their little children to kick him and spit on him.

I could see, too, that he was beginning to slow up. With each small movement, his every muscle flexed as if he were running a race. He was shaking . . . but he kept pushing on . . . slowly.

And then he fell. Of course, the crowd mocked and mimicked and screamed their bold threats and talked their vulgar talk.

He got up and started again, but after that, he just kept collapsing under the weight of the cross. Finally, they permitted another man to carry it the rest of the way.

We arrived. We were at Golgotha. The soldiers grabbed Jesus and jerked him around and talked real mean as if trying to prove themselves men of great strength and virility.

"Lay him down on the cross."

Several of them started to pull him forward, but he calmly
. . . easily . . . walked right out of their grips and laid himself
down. . . . It was ALL so strange that way.

And then—

How I wish I hadn't been looking! Or listening! The nails
. . . huge spikes . . . they drove them into his hands—right
through the palms of his hands. I still shudder.

There was the sound of metal banging on metal . . . and the
background of cheers. There were a few sobs . . . from ladies
. . . and at moments—eerie moments—silence.

From this man Jesus, though, only a small cry. But it ex-
pressed SO much agony and suffering.

They pounded again. His eyes filled with tears; his face was
drawn. His whole body was twisted in severe and acute pain.

I finally had to turn around . . . I couldn't take the sight of
him anymore. The soldiers faithfully finished their task, I
guess.

Next thing I knew, the cross was up, standing securely.

There he hung. Men and women were laughing, pointing,
jeering, spitting, and being sick comedians. The soldiers who
had just driven the spikes were gambling over his robe.

There he hung, nails piercing his hands and feet, blood
flowing freely . . . and life flowing with it.

I avoided his face for as long as I could. I don't know why.
But then I looked . . . and I'll never forget that look in his
eyes. It was love; I know it was! He was looking down at the
men who had just nailed him to the cross and loving them . . .
forgiving them. He was looking at the ugly and dirty people
who were spitting and laughing. His eyes read nothing but
love . . . and forgiveness.

He looked at me. Something inside of me wanted to cry out,
"What kind of man are you?"

My heart is still beating crazily.

It's getting really dark now . . . everything's so strange . . .
so eerie.

What am I doing here? I've got to leave this place.

Devotional for Easter Week

Jane K. Priewe

A wooden cross and 1 Corinthians 13 are the basis for this devotion for school-aged youngsters. Use a rustic cross constructed from the bare trunk of a tree. Prior to the service, hammer seven nails into the cross' upright trunk within reach of the children. Love is the theme for this devotion, and the children can conduct the service.

Two weeks before the devotion is to be held, assign one of these words (love, patient, understanding, kind, truthful, forgiving, humble) to seven youngsters. Tell each child to read 1 Corinthians 13 carefully, and to prepare a short speech (no more than 1½ to 2 minutes) on how the assigned word applied to Jesus. (For example, Jesus showed His love by preaching, healing, honoring His mother, forgiving those who were unkind to Him, dying for our sins, etc. Because of this deep love, He was each of the other six words.) What were some of the things He did that showed these traits? The child assigned each word speaks briefly about how Jesus had that one particular trait. Either his teacher or parents may give help with the writing if he needs it.

Prior to devotion time, print each of the seven words on its own card in large, dark letters. Punch a hole at the top so that it can easily be slipped over a nail to hang from the cross.

The following is a format for this devotion which should take no more than fifteen to twenty minutes.

1. All children sing a familiar Easter hymn.
2. Response reading:
   Child reader: I can't speak with the tongues of men and of angels without sounding like a noisy gong or a clanging cymbal,
   Response (all): Unless I have love.
   Reader: Even though I have the gift of prophesy, know all mysteries and all knowledge, I am nothing,
   Response: Unless I have love.
   Reader: Even though I give my possessions to feed the poor, it earns me nothing,

Response: Unless I have love.

Reader: I will not be patient or kind. I will be jealous and arrogant,

Response: Unless I have love.

Reader: I will not be understanding or forgiving,

Response: Unless I have love.

Reader: I will not be truthful or humble,

Response: Unless I have love.

Reader: When I am grown-up, faith, hope, and love will abide in me,

Response: But the greatest of these is love.

3. Child hangs "love" sign at top of cross, and stands beside the cross to speak. Takes seat when finished.
4. Child hangs "patient" sign under the love sign on the cross, and speaks. Takes seat when finished.
5. "Understanding" sign. Same format.
6. "Kind" sign. Same format.
7. "Truthful" sign. Same format.
8. "Forgiving" sign. Same format.
9. "Humble" sign. Same format.
10. Sing another Easter hymn.
11. Cover the cross with a black cloth to symbolize Jesus' death on Good Friday. Two children can cover the cross.
12. Close devotion with the Lord's Prayer. A prayer circle may be formed if the group isn't too large, or assign a child the closing prayer a week before the devotion is to be held.

If I Had Seen . . .

B. J. Hoff

If I had been with Jesus
    and had seen Him crucified,
I think I would have trembled,
    and I know I would have cried;

If I had been there, watching,
    as they took Him from the cross,
My heart would have been broken
    with the pain of grief and loss;

But if I'd been a witness
    as they rolled the stone away
And found our blessed Savior gone
    that glorious Easter Day,

My soul would have rejoiced
    to hear the angel when he said,
"He is not here, for He is risen—
    Risen from the dead!"

The Beauty of the Earth

(Program for Youth and Adult)

Josephine Breeding

(Arrangements of spring flowers would be appropriate on the performing area.)

Congregational Song or Chorus: "This Is My Father's World"

Superintendent or Leader: Truly this is our Father's world. At all seasons His world is great and beautiful. Now, with the coming of spring, we think of two verses from the Song of Solomon: "For, lo, the winter is past, the rain is over and gone; the flowers appear on the earth; the time of the singing of birds is come, and the voice of the turtle is heard in our land" (2:11, 12). On this spring day, the world is attune to fruitage and to flower. Let us be thankful for God's handiwork.

Prayer (by the minister or superintendent): Dear heavenly Father, we thank You for the beauty of the earth. We thank You for the people of Your world—the babies who are coming to bless our homes—the graduates of our high schools and colleges who are preparing to fit into Your great plan. We thank You for the young couples who, particularly at this season, are coming to pledge their vows, filled with trust and hope for the future. We thank You for loving parents, and we thank You for the aged. Grant that they may always keep spring in their hearts. May each of us find work to do that will help to spread Your kingdom on earth. We ask in Jesus' name. Amen.

Recitation: "At Church"
She did not sit like the feeble folk,
But rose with the crowd to sing.

She bravely suppressed the tremor of age
In her proud old heart was spring.

Solo or Chorus: "Fairest Lord Jesus"

Devotion or Reading (teenager): Spring is a very special season for artists, musicians, and poets. People with cre-
ative ability do not just sit idly by and let all this beauty
go to waste. In the past, artists have produced master-
pieces, and artists will always get out the canvas and
brush on days like these. While the artist describes this
beauty on canvas, the composer writes it in song and
great piano compositions. The poet uses only words.
Many of us are familiar with James Russell Lowell's
familiar lines, "What is so rare as a day in June? Then,
if ever, come perfect days." And these lines from
Robert Browning's *Pippa Passes* never grow old:

"The year's at the spring,
And day's at the morn;
Morning's at seven;
The hillside's dew pearled."

These last two lines sum it up:

"God's in His Heaven—
All's right with the world!"

Congregational Song: "For the Beauty of the Earth"

Recitation: "If I Were Spring"

If I were spring I'd come to please
    Those who anticipate me,
Youngsters with their reel and rod,
    Farmers ready to break the sod.
I'd strew new hope and courage along their paths
        untrod,

If I were spring.

If I were spring I'd scatter floods of light
    For tiny babes who need the rays.
They've starved for warmth, and light, and sun
    Throughout the winter days.
For all shut-ins I'd clothe the earth
    In beautiful array;
For them I'd turn December into May,
    If I were spring.

If I were spring I'd bring the old folks cheer,
    With faded eye and feeble tread
They've weathered one more year;
    They look for spring and signs of life,
They still hold it so dear.
    I'd come and gladden them,
And quiet every fear,
    If I were spring.

Solo or Chorus: "How Great Thou Art"

Benediction (minister or leader): Dear God, as we go from this service may we have a renewed appreciation of Your gifts of life, love, and beauty. Guide us in all we do and keep us ever close to You. We ask in Jesus' name. Amen.

The Real Easter Story As Told By Witnesses

(Modern Day Drama)

Lois McClure Braley

CHARACTERS: Announcer, Peter, John, James, Malchus, Young Girl, Pilate, Pilate's Wife, The Centurion, Joseph of Arimathea, Mary Magdalene, Salome, Mary Mother of James, Cleopas, Thomas.

SCENE: Radio Station. Each person can be dressed in suitable clothing for their character.

PROPS: Microphone, Table, Chairs

ANNOUNCER (sitting at table with microphone): We are about to hear the real Easter story. We have with us witnesses to what happened that first Easter Day. But first we would like to interview witnesses to the crucifixion. Our first witness will be Peter, one of the disciples. (Peter steps forward.)

ANNOUNCER: You were one of the followers weren't you?

PETER: Yes, I was.

ANNOUNCER: Can you tell us what happened, just prior to the crucifixion?

PETER: We, that is the disciples and Jesus, had met for the Passover meal. After we had eaten and sung a song, Jesus said He wanted to go to the Garden of Gethsemane. James and John, along with myself, went with Him into the garden. When we arrived He said He would go a little farther and pray while the three of us waited. We must have fallen asleep because the next thing I knew Jesus was shaking my arm and saying, "Peter, couldn't you even stay awake with me one hour?" Again He left us, and once again we fell asleep. He woke us up again saying the same thing, and then He left us for the third time. It was just impossible to keep our eyes open. I'm sure John and James will

15

agree. (Looks toward them and they come forward.) They will tell you what happened next.

JAMES: When Jesus woke us up the third time, He told us He was ready to leave. As we got to our feet we could see lights approaching in the distance, and we could hear many voices. As they neared we were surprised to see Judas Iscariot, one of us, leading the group of people.

JOHN: Jesus stepped forward and asked for whom they were looking. One of the leaders said, "Jesus of Nazareth." Jesus answered, "I am He." Shortly afterwards Judas stepped forward and kissed Jesus on the cheek, and immediately the soldiers surrounded Him.

JAMES: We didn't know what to do. We were surrounded by soldiers and many people.

PETER: I knew what to do! I grabbed a sword and struck out with it, not really caring whom I hit. I cut the ear off of Malchus, the high priest's servant.

ANNOUNCER: Is he here?

PETER: Yes. Right over there. (Points.)

ANNOUNCER: Would you come here please? (Malchus comes to the table.) I notice you have two ears, but Peter says he cut one off. Can you tell us what happened?

MALCHUS: I'm not too sure myself. I felt this sharp pain on the side of my head, and I saw this man with a sword covered with blood. I put my hand to my head and discovered my ear was just hanging. As I stood there, with blood running down my arm, the man we had come to arrest reached out and touched the side of my head, restoring my ear. I still find it hard to believe, but you can see it certainly looks all right, and I can hear out of it.

ANNOUNCER: I don't think I would have believed it if you hadn't told me yourself. Then what happened? (Looks around.)

JOHN: The soldiers arrested Jesus and took Him into the city. I was so frightened I dropped behind the crowd. So did James.

ANNOUNCER (looking over the witnesses): Did anyone see what actually happened after Jesus reached the city?

PETER: When I got to the place where they were going to try Jesus, I got scared. Not only was I scared, but I was also cold. When I saw a fire in the courtyard, I went over to it. While I was standing there, a young girl approached me.

ANNOUNCER: Let's hear what she has to say. (Young girl steps forward.)

YOUNG GIRL: When I saw this man standing near the fire, he looked familiar to me. I recalled seeing him with the man called Jesus. They were walking along the road. When I approached and asked him if he were a follower of Jesus, he said he wasn't. Later another person in the courtyard asked him the same question, and again he denied it. The third time he was asked, he vehemently denied it. At that moment a cock in the courtyard crowed. This man turned and ran from the courtyard, and we didn't see him again. (Returns to her seat.)

ANNOUNCER (turning to Peter): I thought you were a very close friend of Jesus. Why did you deny this?

PETER: I don't know why. I was very frightened by what had happened, and I was afraid. When I was asked if I knew Jesus, I said I did not. After I was asked the third time, and the cock crowed, I remembered Jesus telling me that I would deny Him three times. I was so ashamed that the only thing I could think of doing was to run away and hide. That's what I did. I ran and hid.

ANNOUNCER: Thank you, Peter, James, and John. You may be seated. Next came the trial. We will now have the witnesses to that. Pilate, I think you were the governor at that time. Would you tell us your part in this?

PILATE (stepping forward): They brought Jesus to me in the middle of the night. I could see it was a Jewish affair, so I told them to take Him to their own leaders. They all left and I thought I was rid of them, but it wasn't long before they were back. Apparently no one wanted to handle the case. I took Him inside and talked with

Him alone. I could find nothing wrong with Him. When I told the crowd this, they became unruly and started shouting, "Crucify Him! Crucify Him!" I was afraid of a riot, so I tried to appease them by offering to have Jesus beaten by the soldiers. Even this did not satisfy the mob. I could see that I had very little choice. (Pilate's wife jumps up and rushes forward.)

PILATE'S WIFE: I told him not to have anything to do with this whole thing. I had had a dream and it frightened me. I knew there was something special about Jesus, but he (pointing at Pilate) just wouldn't listen to me.

ANNOUNCER (addressing Pilate): Is this true?

PILATE: Yes. She did warn me. But what was I to do? The mob was out of control by this time, and it looked like the only thing that would satisfy them was the crucifixion of Jesus. However, I did try something. I thought it might be the solution to the whole problem. Every year at Passover time I release a prisoner. In the jail there was a notorious robber and murderer named Barabbas. I hoped that if I offered to release Barabbas or Jesus they would be frightened enough to take Jesus and let Him go free. How was I to know they would continue to scream for the crucifixion of Jesus?

ANNOUNCER: So you released a known criminal and condemned an innocent man to death!

PILATE: What was I to do? I knew He was innocent. I even told the crowd this, but they wouldn't listen. They just shouted louder and louder, "Crucify Him! Crucify Him!" The only thing I could do was turn Him over to them, and then wash my hands of the whole mess. (Wrings hands.) But I can't get my hands clean! I condemned an innocent man to death. What could I do? (Returns to seat.)

ANNOUNCER (looking at witnesses): Do we have anyone who saw what happened next?

CENTURION (coming forward): I was one of the soldiers who took Jesus to Golgotha for the crucifixion. Before we started the soldiers beat Him, spat in His face, and ridiculed Him. They finally put a crown of thorns on

His head and placed a cross on His back. By this time He was exhausted, and while we were walking along the road He stumbled. The first time He was able to get back on His feet, but He stumbled again. That time we could see it was going to be impossible for Him to get up. In the crowd that was lined up along the road we saw a big man. One of the soldiers reached out and grabbed him, telling him to carry the cross.

ANNOUNCER: Is he here?

CENTURION: Yes. I believe his name is Simon of Cyrene.

ANNOUNCER: Simon, would you come forward please? (Simon approaches.) Would you tell us what happened?

SIMON: I was just standing there with the crowd, wondering what had caused it to gather. Then I saw the soldiers, and in the middle of them I saw a man carrying a cross. He stumbled a couple of times. When He couldn't get up the second time, I noticed the soldiers looking around. One of them came to me and grabbed my arm. He told me to carry the cross. As I bent to take it from the fallen man, He looked at me as if to say thank you. I carried it the rest of the way.

ANNOUNCER: Thank you. (Simon returns to seat.) What happened next?

CENTURION: When we arrived at Golgotha we made ready for the crucifixion. There were two men, robbers, that were crucified at the same time. We put them on either side of Jesus. We had orders to put a sign over Jesus' head that read THIS IS JESUS KING OF THE JEWS.
While we were waiting for the three of them to die, some of the soldiers threw dice for the robe of Jesus. Also, it suddenly became dark like the night. This lasted from noon until three. Everyone was very frightened. Suddenly Jesus shouted from the cross. We could hear every word He said. He shouted, "MY GOD! MY GOD! WHY HAVE YOU FORSAKEN ME?" Once He seemed to look directly at me as He said, "Forgive them as they don't know what they are doing." Again He shouted with a loud voice and there

was a terrible earthquake. I threw myself to my knees. As I looked up at this man hanging on the cross, I realized He had to be the Son of God.

ANNOUNCER: Did He die at this time?

CENTURION: Yes. When we were told to break His legs to hasten death, we discovered that He was already dead.

ANNOUNCER: I understand a friend requested the body. Was it one of you? (Looks at the witnesses; man comes forward.)

JOSEPH OF ARIMATHEA: I am Joseph of Arimathea. I was a follower of Jesus. Knowing of the death of Jesus, I thought about the tomb I had prepared for myself. I was willing to use it for the body of Jesus. I sent a servant to Pilate requesting the body. After he made sure that Jesus was dead, Pilate granted my request. I asked Nicodemus to help me. We wrapped the body in cloth, and, while Mary and Mary Magdalene watched, we placed it in the tomb. When we were finished, a huge rock was placed in front of the opening. At the request of the Jewish leaders, Pilate put guards on duty. I guess they were afraid someone would take the body and say He had risen. (Returns to seat.)

ANNOUNCER: We will now skip the events of the next couple days. It is now Easter Sunday. I understand the women played a prominent part in these events. Would one of you tell us what happened? (Mary, Mary Magdalene, and Salome step forward.)

MARY MAGDALENE: I'm Mary Magdalene. Mary, Salome, and I were up early that morning. We hadn't slept much since Jesus' death. The whole experience had been such a shock. We had purchased spices and were taking them to the tomb.

SALOME: We were walking along discussing the events of the past few days. All of a sudden we remembered the huge stone that had been placed in front of the tomb. We wondered among ourselves how we were going to move it.

MARY: As we neared the tomb we were surprised to see the

stone had been rolled from the front. Also we noticed that the soldiers were gone. We started running toward the tomb, because we were afraid someone might have stolen the body.

MARY MAGDALENE: We entered the tomb, and there on the right sat an angel clothed in white. We were frightened, but the angel told us not to be. He said that Jesus was not there, but that He had risen just as He said He would. He told us to look at the place where Jesus had been. All we found were the clothes He had been wrapped in. The angel told us to go quickly and tell the disciples about what we had seen. We were also to tell them to go to Galilee where Jesus would meet them.

MARY: We quickly ran to the disciples and told them. Peter and John rushed to the tomb.

PETER (stepping forward): We were stunned when the women told us about the angel, and not finding Jesus' body in the tomb. John and I rushed to the tomb to see for ourselves. We found it just as the women had said. Immediately we left for Galilee.

MARY MAGDALENE: As soon as they had left, I returned to the tomb. I thought maybe I might find out something more. When I got there, the angel was no longer there. As I was sitting near the tomb I started to cry. I heard someone behind me. When I turned I saw a man. I thought he must be the gardener, so I asked him if he had removed the body of Jesus. If he had, I asked if he would please tell me where he had put Him. The man spoke to me, and all he said was, "Mary." Immediately I knew it was Jesus. I ran to Him and fell on my knees. As I reached out to touch Him, He stepped backwards and told me not to touch Him. I knew without a doubt it was Jesus, my Lord.

ANNOUNCER: Did anyone else see Jesus at this time?

CLEOPAS (stepping forward): Yes, I did. A companion and I were walking along the road to Emmaus when suddenly Jesus was walking with us. At that time we didn't know who He was. He asked us why we were so sad so we told Him about the crucifixion. It was getting late when we neared the village, so we invited

Him to dine with us. When He blessed and broke the bread during the meal, then we recognized Him.

PETER (stepping forward again): On another occasion we were all gathered together when suddenly Jesus was with us.

THOMAS (jumping up): I wasn't there that time. When the disciples told me they had seen Jesus, I didn't believe them. I told them the only way I would believe was to put my hands in the nailprints in His hands and feet. Later, though, we were all together and Jesus appeared again. Somehow He knew that I had doubted the fact that He was alive. He showed me the nailprints and told me to touch them. I believed. (Returns to seat.)

JOHN: Later He appeared while we were fishing. We had fished all night and had caught nothing. At dawn we saw a man standing on the beach. We couldn't see whom He was. He called to us and asked if we had caught any fish. When we said that we had not, He told us to put our net over the right side of the boat, and we would get fish. We did as He said and caught so many fish we couldn't draw in the net. I turned to Peter and said, "It is the Lord." Peter immediately jumped into the water and swam to the shore. The rest of us rowed the boat to shore, dragging the net of fish. When we landed, we found a fire with fish and bread that Jesus had fixed for us. What fellowship we had with Jesus that day.

ANNOUNCER (as all the witnesses take their seats): Thank you. We have heard actual witnesses to the crucifixion and resurrection of Jesus. I think we have proved that Jesus did die, but that He also rose from the dead. It is this fact of the resurrection that makes Easter. Without it we would not have life after death. Truly this was the Son of God. As He said to Thomas, "You believe because you have seen Me, but blessed are those who haven't seen Me and believe anyway."

SONG: "He lives"

PENTECOST

Power at Pentecost

(Program for Pentecost)

Florence Harper Haney

PARTICIPANTS: Prayer Reader
     5 Bible Readers
     Group Readers
     Youth choir or soloists (optional)
     (All music may be sung by congregation.)
Organ Prelude: "Spirit of God, Descend Upon My Heart"
Prayer Poem:
     Spirit of God, descend upon my heart;

     Wean it from earth, through all its pulses move;

     Stoop to my weakness, mighty as Thou art,

     And make me love Thee as I ought to love.

     Teach me to feel that Thou art always nigh;

     Teach me the struggles of the soul to bear,

     To check the rising doubt, the rebel sigh;

     Teach me the patience of unanswered prayer.
                        In Jesus' name. Amen.

1—Coming of the Spirit

Bible Reader 1: When the day of Pentecost had come, they were all together in one place. And suddenly there came from heaven a noise like a violent, rushing wind, and it filled the whole house where they were sitting. And there appeared to them tongues as of fire distributing themselves, and they rested on each one of them. And they were all filled with the Holy Spirit and began to speak with other tongues, as the Spirit was giving them utterance (Acts 2:1-4, A.S.V.).

Hymn: "Old-Time Power" (We are gathered for Thy blessing.)

2—Every Nation Marvels

Bible Reader 2: Now there were Jews living in Jerusalem, devout men, from every nation under heaven. And when this sound occurred, the multitude came together, and were bewildered, because they were each one hearing them speak in his own language. And they were amazed and marveled, saying, "Why, are not all these who are speaking Galileans? And how is it that we each hear them in our own language to which we were born? . . . we hear them in our own tongues speaking of the mighty deeds of God." And they continued in amazement and great perplexity, saying to one another, "What does this mean?" (Acts 2:5-8, 11, 12, A.S.V.).

Hymn: "Pentecostal Power" (Lord, as of old at Pentecost Thou didst Thy power display.)

3—Peter Proclaims God's Message

Bible Reader 3: But Peter, taking his stand with the eleven, raised his voice and declared to them: "Men of Judea, and all you who live in Jerusalem, let this be known to you, and give heed to my words . . . this is what was spoken of through the prophet Joel: 'And it shall be in the last days,' God says, 'That I will pour forth of My Spirit upon all mankind; and your sons and your daughters shall prophesy, and your young men shall see visions, and your old men shall dream dreams; even upon My bondslaves, both men and women, I will in those days pour forth of My Spirit and they shall prophesy . . . And it shall be, that every one who calls on the name of the Lord shall be saved' " (Acts 2:14), 16-18, 21, A.S.V.).

Hymn: "O Breath of Life" (O Breath of Life, come sweeping through us.)

4—Peter Calls for Repentance

Bible Reader 4: Now when they heard this, they were pierced to the heart, and said to Peter and the rest of the apostles, "Brethren, what shall we do?" And Peter said to them, "Repent, and let each of you be baptized in the name of Jesus Christ for the forgiveness of your sins; and you shall receive the gift of the Holy Spirit. For the promise is for you and your children, and for all who are far off, as many as the Lord our God shall call to Himself" (Acts 2:37-39, A.S.V.).

Hymn: "Thy Holy Spirit, Lord, Alone" (Thy Holy Spirit, Lord, alone can turn our hearts from sin.)

5—The Church Begins

Bible Reader 5: So then, those who had received his word were baptized; and there were added that day about three thousand souls. And they were continually devoting themselves to the apostles' teaching and to fellowship, to the breaking of bread and to prayer . . . And day by day continuing with one mind in the temple, and breaking bread from house to house, they were taking their meals together with gladness and sincerity of heart, praising God, and having favor with all the people. And the Lord was adding to their number day by day those who were being saved" (Acts 2:41, 42, 46, 47, A.S.V.).

Choral Reading: "Prepare Us for Power"
Group 1: *P*repare us for your great power,
Group 2:   Spirit from on high.
Group 1: *E*nter every humble heart with cleansing fire,
Group 2:   Flame that will not die.

Group 1: *N*aming Christ's name above every other name,
Group 2:   What joy fills us now!
Group 1: *T*each us truth, O faithful guide. Turn us from sin.
Group 2:   Trusting now, we bow.
Group 1: *E*quip the church to sing God's endless mercies,
Group 2:   O heavenly love.
Group 1: *C*omforting promise of the Father, come now,
Group 2:   Call our thoughts above.
Group 1: *O*ver our souls pour out thy refining fire,
Group 2:   Let thy pure light shine.
Group 1: *S*peak through the mighty, rushing wind of God's Word,
Group 2:   O Spirit divine.
Group 1: *T*ogether we will sing triumphant tidings:
Group 2:   Savior, we are Thine!

(Note: If desired, posters may be made with letters spelling out "Pentecost." These can be turned toward the congregation as appropriate phrases are read.)

Closing Hymn: "Revive Us Again"

A Service for Pentecost

(Departmental Program)

Jane K. Priewe

Program Information:

This service is geared for departmental participation and takes little practice. Group 1 (Grade 4) handles the introduction. Give each child one short line to read or recite. For a smaller group, give each child more than one line.

Group 2 (Grade 6), Group 3 (Grades 7 & 8), and Group 4 (Grade 5) should run through their parts a couple of times in order to coordinate sound effects and banner or poster raising with readers' parts. Group 4 (Grade 5) will be in charge of making banners or posters and holding them. (Discuss banners or posters with the children who will make them at least three weeks before Pentecost, and check each Sunday to be sure they're in the process of being constructed.) Banners or posters should be displayed from the front. Group 3 can remain seated while they produce specific sound effects, which must be practiced a couple of weeks before the service. Readers can work in front of the audience near the banners.

Group 5 (Grade 3) introduces and leads the birthday song. Since it's an easy song, and youngsters are familiar with the tune to "Happy Birthday," a practice the Sunday before Pentecost should be enough. Banner holders from Group 4 should practice with singers at this time, because the older children will need the words to sing along.

Teachers and/or girls from Group 3 are in charge of baking a birthday cake and making sure there are enough bird-shaped cookies for each child to have a cookie at the end of the service. (Use a favorite recipe for the cookies.) The cake can be given to the person who happens to be sitting in a particular chair which was marked with tape or string before the children assembled.

27

Program

Opening Prayer: By minister, teacher, or child

Song: "Holy Spirit, Faithful Guide"

Group 1: (Voices)
> Why aren't we having regular Sunday school today?
> Yeah, why are we meeting here?
> We're supposed to have a special program.
> Why? What's so special about today?
> It's Pentecost.
> Pentecost! What's that?
> I know it comes after Easter.
> But what is it? What happened on Pentecost?
> I think it's when lots of people became Christians.
> I never heard of Pentecost. Where can I read about it?
> The whole story of Pentecost is in Acts 2.
> Good! Let's see what it says!

Group 2 (Readers) **Group 3** (Sound effects) **Group 4** (Make and hold banners)

Reader 1: The Day of Pentecost came, and Jesus' disciples were gathered together in a room. Suddenly, a noise like a rushing wind came from Heaven. The noise filled the whole building.
(Rushing wind sound effect, and a child from Group 4 holds up a banner showing swirling wind to the audience.)

Reader 2: Tongues of flames came from each disciple, and they spoke all kinds of unfamiliar languages, because each man was filled with the power of the Holy Spirit.
(Sound effect of voices speaking different languages, and a child holds up a banner showing a large flame.)

Reader 3: Many Jews who lived in Jerusalem but came from other countries, heard the disciples speaking in their native languages. They couldn't understand how all of a sudden the disciples could speak in other tongues. These men had never been away from the Holy Land!

28

Reader 4: Some people laughed and mocked the disciples. They even accused them of drinking too much wine. Peter raised his voice and shouted, "We have *not* been drinking wine! Who'd drink wine this early in the day?"

Reader 5: "You're forgetting what God said through the prophet Joel," Peter continued. "He said that in the last days He'd pour His Spirit on all men. He said we'd prophesy, see visions, and dream dreams. He said we'd see wonders in the sky, signs on earth, and that everyone who accepted Jesus would be saved."
(Child from Group 4 holds up banner with words, "Holy Spirit" on it.)

Reader 6: The people gathered around the disciples murmured, but Peter raised his voice and they stopped to listen. "Men of Israel!" Peter shouted, "You've seen Jesus of Nazareth perform miracles and wonders. You know He was crucified, and that God raised Him from the dead, because death had no power over Him."

Reader 7: Peter continued: "David knew the Messiah would come some day. He said the Lord was always at his right hand. David was happy, because he knew that through the Christ he'd be saved and would go to heaven. Never doubt that! The man you crucified, Jesus of Nazareth, *is* the Christ!"
(People murmur. Sound effects saying, "What shall we do? What can we do? Help us! What's the answer?" etc. While they continue to mutter, a child from Group 4 holds up a banner showing a stream or pool of water.)

Reader 8: Peter told the people they should repent, and be baptized in the name of Jesus Christ for the forgiveness of their sins. He said if they would do this they would receive the gift of the Holy Spirit. Many people did believe him, and about three thousand were baptized that day.
(Banners can remain raised throughout the rest of the service.)

Song: "Open My Eyes, That I May See"

Group 5: (One child speaks.) Pentecost is really the birthday of the church. After we sing this song all the way through, will you all join in as we sing the four verses a second time?
(After little ones have sung the verses, Group 5 youngsters raise banners with these words written on them.)

    1. A wind blew that day,
         On Pentecost Day,
         We knew God was near,
         A wind blew that day.

    2. Tongues of flame came that day,
         On Pentecost Day,
         Filled men with the Holy Spirit,
         Tongues of flame came that day.

    3. Repent, be baptized
         Said Peter that day,
         In the name of our Savior,
         Repent, be baptized.

    4. Happy birthday to you
         On Pentecost Day,
         Happy birthday, dear church,
         Happy birthday to you.

(When this song is sung, a child from Group 5 carries a birthday cake—lighted candles if legal and safe—to the front, and holds it while the children sing.) Find out who gets the birthday cake (claimed *after* service is concluded).

Closing prayer: By pastor, teacher, or child

Pass out cookies shaped like a bird.

MOTHER'S DAY

Mother . . .

Her heart is our companion all through life . . .
Her faith, our quiet partner in success . . .
Her strength, our constant anchor in the storm . . .
Her love, our greatest joy throughout the years.

B. J. Hoff

Mother's Day Blessing

Ralphine Jacobs

God bless you, Mother,
The young and brave, so full of charms,
With your firstborn cradled in your arms.
You struggle with formulas, fevers, and frets,
And the countless fears no young mother forgets;
Yet you face the future with undaunted cheer,
Growing with your children through each hectic year.

God bless you, Mother,
The mature, with the wisdom of experienced years,
Patient and steadfast through toil and tears;
You cope with the whims and foibles of youth
With infallible weapons—love, faith, and truth,
Guiding your young ones, showing the way
For them to be leaders themselves, one day.

God bless you, Mother,
The aged and careworn, the feeble and slow,
Who lean on your children as onward you go,
Though wrinkled, still charming to daughter or son,
For your unselfish ways, for the good you have done.
To the end of your journey, to the last of your days,
God bless you, Mother, God bless you always.

Gifts for Mother's Day

(Two Act Play for Older Teenagers)

Hazel Bacon

Properties: Act 1—Ten chairs for special meeting. Act 2—Add table or desk, and rearrange to look like an office.

Cast: Judy Ingram (strong leader of the group)
Rex Nolten (also a strong leader)
Susan Andrews (faithful member)
Tom Elsworth (faithful member)
Ellen O'Brien (faithful member)
Joe Crist (faithful member)
Ruth Darling (faithful member)
Bobby Mason (faithful member)
Mr. Stokes (minister)

Act 1

(Judy Ingram and Rex Nolten walk into the meeting slowly. Now and then Judy studies her notebook and uses her pencil.)

JUDY: We have so little time, Rex. If our minister REALLY wants another play . . .

REX: Just SOMETHING for Mother's Day is being talked about, Judy.

JUDY: Yes, but we have only two weeks.

SUSAN (entering): What is this meeting all about? (Sits after speaking.)

TOM: I hope NOT a play. I have too much schoolwork.

ELLEN (walks in alone): Our minister is coming. I just met him.

JOE (sits near Ellen): Play rehearsals take too much time.

JUDY: If it IS a play, Joe, we mustn't let our minister down. He's O.K.

REX: I agree. He's a great guy—works hard.

(Bobby and Ruth enter and are seated. They're followed by a

32

smiling, pleasant Mr. Stokes, who stands before them.)

MR. STOKES: Thank you young people for coming. You've always done excellent work on short notice. However, this request is different, and there's not much time.

In making house calls, I have realized that about thirty active church mothers are those with the most children—our largest families. I have also realized that grandmothers are mothers, too, and some of ours are not in very good health. But THEY are the ones who help to make our church dinners and special occasions great successes. I want them to KNOW we all appreciate their willingness to help whenever they can.

If you young people could sacrifice two Saturday mornings, not BEFORE Mother's Day, but AFTER Mother's Day, from 9 until 12 noon, I think we could show them our appreciation. For those two Saturdays, you would offer your services in their homes, in various ways.

I've made a list of those you could help, and I'll ask Judy and Rex to add your loving services to my list of names. (Takes list from pocket and hands it to Rex—then looks around the group.) I know we have more in this group. Get in touch with them—SOON. I'll leave the details of this home adventure in your hands. Work it out in your own way—by Mother's Day!

Now (looks around at them), I believe I have shared everything. Do I need to worry about it?

PART OF GROUP: No, Mr. Stokes!

REST OF GROUP: Of course not!

MR. STOKES (grinning): Do I hear any groans?

RUTH: Only a few. Your idea may even be FUN.

MR. STOKES: Good! (Turns toward the door.)

TOM (laughingly): As long as our service to others doesn't rob me of playing tennis.

JOE: I have to take Dad's old car apart, but you can count on me for TWO Saturdays.

MR. STOKES (smiling): Boys, can you imagine Jesus' disciples saying, "We'd rather go fishing!" when He asked them to do something?

TOM (smiling): I GET it. O.K.

JOE: Don't worry, Mr. Stokes.

MR. STOKES: I won't. (Nods and leaves quickly.)

SUSAN: Say, I didn't realize there were such LARGE families in our church.

BOBBY: Just for fun, let's count the families right here. (He motions and ALL move over closer. They could sit on the floor.)

JUDY (after they move): Just give number of children. I'll begin. Two children in my family.

REX: One—I'm an only child.

SUSAN: Four.

TOM: Four.

ELLEN: Seven—in MY house.

JOE: Three.

RUTH: Three.

BOBBY: Eight.

REX: Wow! Thirty-two children in these eight families.

RUTH: Someone can help ME while Mother has a long nap. I bet she'll accept our gifts of service.

JUDY: I believe we will all love these new experiences, when we get started. (Reads her notebook.) Do you realize THIS will take a lot less time than a PLAY?

Now, gang, since this is something new—going into homes to SERVE them—we must remember our manners (looks around), all of us. This project is a good test. You ALL know what Mr. Stokes said about "We'd rather go fishing!"
What we have promised to do will be an example of Christ's love on earth for each other—old or young (smiles). No gossiping allowed in any form. Right?

SUSAN: It is. Right now we need a prayer to guide us, and hold us to our promises, as we meet all kinds of situations with mothers. Rex, YOUR turn.

REX (most seriously): Lord Jesus, show us how You want us to serve. Give us loving hearts and patience in ALL we do. Help us not to fail Mr. Stokes, or YOU, Lord, or the rest of our group. Amen.

JUDY: Susan and Ruth, will you assist me in phoning? Here are some names and numbers of our mothers I've written down. (Tears out pages on which she has written. They accept them.)

Please explain to them what our minister said tonight. Tell them that their lists are NEEDED at our meeting BEFORE church THIS coming Sunday. O.K.? Also we will call other members of our group who are not here and enlist their help in our project.

Act 2

(Four weeks later)

Cast: Same, but after school, about 4 P.M. (Some carry books.)

Office: Mr. Stokes sits at his desk, busy with his books and papers.

NOTE: Costumes should be changed. A coat, on or off, would save time.

JUDY (carrying her same little notebook): We came to report.

MR. STOKES (looking up from his work): Hello, there! I called all the active members of your group. I wanted reports of your services in the homes of our church mothers who signed up with their special needs. (Shows enthusiasm.) Now—how did it go?

JUDY: GREAT! The Lord surely gave YOU a wonderful idea in asking us to share some of OUR time with others.

MR. STOKES: I am glad you said the Lord THROUGH me, for that means the Lord through ALL of you.

REX: Yeah—we may ALL get into trouble. I hear the fathers of our church would like to have MORE of such home services for their Father's Day gifts.

MR. STOKES (laughing): Well, we won't worry about THAT! Judy, will you report on those who helped in THIS group but cannot report today?

JUDY (reading from her book): Five of our missing members are in school activities today. Two others have part-time work. They are all sorry they cannot be here to report for themselves.

MR. STOKES: I understand those seven did their part in such things as cutting grass, weeding gardens, washing windows for old Mrs. Bradley, and sitting with the sick. God bless them all.

Well, Judy, what is your own personal report?

JUDY (smiling—points to self): ME? Mr. Stokes, I never thought I could be a mother's helper or a nurse, but I SURE got into BOTH. As you know, twenty-one of our church members had service requests for IN their homes. I stayed with Mrs. Russell's mother so she could take her three younger children for new shoes. As it turned out, I served luncheon for ALL those left at home. I even helped the year old baby to walk— besides the mending.

REX: Good girl! MY turn! Well, I tackled things I never did before—like sawing boards and mixing paint. I even put up a new clothesline for Mrs. Milly Smith. I remembered she had lost her husband, and, believe me, those five children keep her very busy.

(LOUD knocks are heard on door—voices. The other six have come. They open door and they speak all at once.)

TOM: Hi! Mr. Stokes!

SUSAN: We came to report.

ELLEN: Judy, we're here!

JOE: Hello, Rex!

RUTH: Sorry to be late.

BOBBY: Where shall we put our books?

MR. STOKES (hand up for silence): Put your books over there. I will not keep you long. I want to hear your reports on services rendered in our Mother's Day project.

Susan, tell us about it. (He makes notes.) How did you spend your time?

SUSAN: I went to Mrs. Ronald Briggs—both Saturdays. I

36

took the two younger children to the dentist. It was exciting.

REX: To the DENTIST?

SUSAN: Yes—and we did food shopping on the way home! The next week I had to entertain twelve children who came too early for Jennie Briggs' birthday party. Mrs. Briggs had to go pick up the cake. I really had a GOOD time. I felt ten years younger, but I DID work overtime.

ELLEN: MY experiences were in FOUR homes—MOSTLY the Brock families. I had to sew buttons on, mend stockings, socks, curtains, and wash dishes—but they were all so loving and grateful.

RUTH: My hours of work were mostly out-of-doors. I went on store errands twice—to get money back from things bought by that big Ellis family—things that were the wrong size—or not wanted. It sounds difficult, but they had ALL saved the sales slips so—I just collected their money, like they said. They were so pleasant and grateful. Mrs. Ellis has two grandmothers and nine children.

MR. STOKES: A great story, Ruth. Your turn, Tom.

TOM (laughing): My story is far from my tennis hobby, Mr. Stokes. Believe it or not, I washed windows, chopped wood for the Bennet's fireplace, and . . . guess what? I was called upon to pull out a tooth. Little Marcia Bennet had tied a string on her first loose tooth. Her mother and Marcia BOTH asked me to pull it.

REX: Brave man!

MR. STOKES: Next—Joe!

JOE (speaking slowly, looking around): I'm still surprised and touched about MY story. You know that little old lady, Mrs. Miller's sister? She asked me just to sit with her and read her Bible—out loud. She has bad eyes. The second Saturday—if she didn't call me back, again! Same thing! We got past Matthew, Mark, half of John, then some of the beautiful Psalms. I bet the Lord had a hand in THAT. Time goes fast when you read to somebody who REALLY listens.

MR. STOKES: Bless you, Joe. You responded well! Bobby!

BOBBY: I had to write some LETTERS. Just like I was a secretary—then to the post office. At the next place I had to call a doctor for a sick baby. That was the Wilson baby. Their phone was out of order. One more thing—I put a washer in their kitchen faucet. I don't know why, but all of that makes a fellow feel good.

MR. STOKES: Your reports let me know that you young disciples have right attitudes. God bless you all.
Now—I know you are in a hurry, but ONE more thing. In each new experience we can benefit, if we remember as we should. I want each of you to give me a one sentence summary of what those two Saturdays of service to others meant to you. I'll give you one minute to think. (Walks back and forth as they think—takes down what they say.)
Well—Judy!

JUDY: I loved all of the work I did, but I KNOW I need more patience.

REX: I am stronger when thinking of others first and self last.

SUSAN: I now have confidence to do more new things. It was—exciting!

ELLEN: I learned that older people are REALLY interesting.

RUTH: I have more love for people and their problems.

TOM: Since I pulled Marcia Bennet's tooth, I *think* I will be—a dentist.

JOE: I cannot forget how GOOD it felt to read that Bible to old Mrs. Miller's sister.

BOBBY: There is great satisfaction to work WELL for others. I felt GOOD. I still do!

MR. STOKES: (Reaches out. All hold hands in a circle.)

ALL (glancing at each other): God be with me and thee, while we are absent one from the other. Amen.

MR. STOKES (looking at watch): Now back to my desk. Thank you all for reporting.

Curtain

Patchwork Quilt Banquet

(Mother-Daughter Banquet Program)

Elvera Wilken

Materials: Many wrapping papers and materials in fabric are available in patchwork design. Use these for place-mats, booklet covers, nut cups, or centerpieces. Favors of sewing implements (thimbles, needles, rippers, hem rulers, etc.) could be wrapped in patchwork paper.

If divided paper plates are used, these, too, can look patchwork. Serve different colors of food in each section: buttered carrots (orange), potatoes (white), buttered peas or beans (green), ham (red), and perhaps a yellow lemon salad. Dessert could be rainbow sherbet and cookies.

Program

Song: "Faith of Our Mothers"

Devotions: 1 Corinthians 12:17, 18, 20 (Older mother has devotions.) How like a patchwork quilt our lives are. Each little piece alone is so useless and serves such a little purpose. But set together in proper place, fastened securely, each piece functions well. A quilt, as well as our bodies, can be very useful.

People, congregations, organizations, and families must be fitted together, work together, pull together—secured by love. If each one is totally independent and strives to pull alone, very little can be accomplished. All must work for a common good. Each must diligently fill his own little spot, with his eye on a common goal for the good of all.

Prayer: Thank you, dear Lord, for putting our bodies together in such an intricate pattern. May each part function properly, that we may serve You to the fullest. Amen.

Little Girl: (A little girl who can speak and sing well sits in a small rocker with doll and small quilt.)

When Melinda Sue gets fussy
  With a tummy ache or cold,
I love her and pat her (hugs and pats doll),
  And never, never scold.

I wrap her tight and keep her warm
  In her little patchwork quilt (wraps dolly).
Rock-a-bye my dolly
  While I sing a little lilt.
(She rocks as she sings a lullaby.)

Mother: "My Quilt"
As you so calmly view my quilt, of red and green and
    blue,
It seems a jumbled lot of goods and tangled floss to
    you.
This piece of bright red calico—to you means nothing
    more—
To me—it's my first day at school. I'm six years old
    once more.
This tiny piece of yellowed white—to me has much to
    say,
For I'm a blushing bride once more, and this—my
    wedding day.
This dainty piece of pink and white bids all past years
    depart,
My firstborn baby lies once more close to its mother's
    heart.
So woven all through my quilt are many days of life:
The high days and the holidays, the days of joy and
    strife.
And when I leave God's earth below to cross death's
    narrow sea,
I'll wrap these memories round my soul and take them
    home with me.

Teenager: "When Grandma Comes"
When Grandma comes to our house,
  Quiet steps and walking slow,

She finds a sunny corner—
　Rocks in her rocker to-and-fro.

But her hands are never idle,
　For she asks for Mother's scraps,
Carefully she takes each one
　And lays them in her lap.

And then she reminisces
　To days that have been,
Of garments she or Mother made
　For special moments then.

"Now this is Susan's concert dress,
　And this is Johnny's shirt.
This piece of white a collar, dear,
　And this your aqua skirt."

She lovingly caresses each
　As though they understand.
Each one to her a precious gem
　As she holds them in her hand.

With deft precision then she cuts
　A piece of pink or blue.
As she stitches them together
　A pattern comes to view.

Each block is a bit of history
　From the life of some loved one,
And she lives a life all over
　Until each block is done.

When all the blocks are finished,
　And put together row on row,
They are more than little pieces—
　There is life—and love—aglow.

Speaker: (Any mother who speaks well.)
　Every life is very complex and can be compared to
　some of the very complex patterns of a patchwork
　quilt. Each life is made up of many and varied compo-

nents, even as a quilt is made up of many and varied pieces. Each life contains various amounts of certain characteristics just as quilts contain more of one color than another.

Some of life's pieces are:

1. Ability. Perhaps this should be green (display a green square), for green depicts growth, accomplishment, and achievement. Colossians 2:19 says: "Holding fast to the head (Jesus), from whom the entire body, being supplied and held together by the joints and ligaments, grows with a growth which is from God." We are dependent on Christ for strength to grow, to accomplish, and to achieve. Green is a color for ability, for it blends with other colors. Just look at any flower garden.

2. Temperament. This varies much in each person, but let's use a piece of tan. It goes with bright colors and also with some grey colors. (Display a piece of tan material.)

Tan is the average life. No one is pure and perfect. Every life is a little "off-color" or tainted by sin. Temperament means how do we adjust to situations. Do we become angry when we do not get our way? Are we moody and not talking? Are we middle-of-the-road and unable to make decisions? Do we become jealous and envious when someone gets things we cannot afford? Are we angry when we are not the winner? These are the grey prints in our tan life. Or are we able to laugh at our own mistakes? Can we offer encouragement to a loser? Can we praise people? Do we feel joy for others? Can we smile at all we meet? These are the bright colors in our tan life.

3. Countenance (a grey piece of material). Do we look like this? With a sad and discontented looking face? Do we find fault with everyone and everything? Do we feel dejected all the time? Do we look on the dark side of every endeavor? Do we gripe when the sun shines (It's too hot!), and gripe when the clouds come (It's too cool!). Then we DO look like this grey piece. Or is our countenance one of smiles, joy, happiness? Do we brighten a room when we come in? Do we smile at people, greet people, and shake their hands? Do we see and dwell upon the good that can come from any given undertaking? Are folks glad to have us around? Then we represent this piece (a very bright color).

4. Many pieces are not very usable. (Show a piece with a hole in it.) Do we resemble this? Many lives are not usable because they think that way. They imagine and dwell upon their weak points, until they actually do become useless. They have negative reactions to everything, and NO will to rise above this condition.

5. Others are maimed or crippled, but NEVER down. There is always SOMETHING they can do. Maybe they are in wheelchairs, on crutches, or walking with canes, but they do what they can, and are ever aspiring to do more. Many are limbless, sightless, or deaf—yet they are using God-given strengths to perform useful duties. Their life has been patched (show cloth with a sturdy patch), but they are useful to themselves and their fellowmen.

6. Some of us lead lives of hard work. This piece can depict the lives that lack material necessities (piece of denim). Even though they are knocked by trials and toils, covered with grime and dirt, they can come through purged, cleansed, and renewed, and still be strong and bright. A strong and enduring faith will help us to endure in times like these.

7. Some pieces resemble the rich and affluent (piece of silk). They represent a life of ease. Sometimes these pieces are coveted and envied, but they are not always sturdy and useful. They really aren't the desire of the average, normal person. It is better to feel your worth, to know you live a life of service and are an answer to someone's need.

8. The most beautiful is a prayerful life (piece of pure white). These lives are in communion with God, are forgiven by God, and therefore are as nearly perfect as lives can be here on earth. Troubles are eased, heartaches are lessened, lives are strengthened. (Show piece of white with a colored stripe going both ways.) The stripes up and down represent praise to God in thankfulness for blessings they received and for trials they did not receive. Stripes across show prayers of intercession for their fellowmen. They never feel alone, for they have encompassed the whole world with their compassions, and God has promised to be with them unto the end.

You see, each of us is different! We are complex—yet God's way can shine through if we allow it. But we need a perfect pattern. Did you ever try to make a quilt from an imperfect pattern. The pieces just do not fit. Jesus is our perfect pattern. If we follow Him all the way, the pieces will fit His perfect plan and make a perfect quilt of our lives. There may be trials, discouragements, and difficulties, but these will only help to bring out the true pattern.

God can take the pieces of any life and use them. Tattered and broken though they may be, He can restore them and make them usable. Sometimes they are so tainted by sin that He must purge and cleanse them before He can use them—even as the pieces must be washed, pressed, and cut before they are usable for a quilt. So yield to God. Let Him take the broken pieces of your life and make something beautiful of it.

Prayer: Dear Lord, help us to see clearly the pattern you have for our lives. May we trust this pattern, follow this pattern, and live this pattern—that NO one will be led astray by our example. Amen.

Older Mother: "Jesus Quilt"
As I look from my kitchen window, across fields of various hues,
I see Jesus' patchwork quilt against skies of azure blue—
A field of green and waving corn, next to an alfalfa field in bloom.
Then a field of golden grain, ready for harvest soon.
There are patches of rolling pastures dotted with sheep and cows,
Some fields are black and barren, because of tractor and plow.
Each piece is neatly featherstitched by a row of posts and wire.

44

I feel a peace and contentment. What more could heart
desire?
For this quilt I see from my kitchen is mine and mine
alone,
Given to me by the Master quilt maker as He increased
the seeds I have sown.
We can use our strength to plant the seed, but without
the sun and rain
Our efforts would be fruitless, and our patchwork quilt
in vain.
I thank God for this handiwork, as over the hillside it
lays,
May I never cease to praise Him and serve Him day by
day.

Drill: (For nine girls. They can put the colored pieces on a
flannel board.)
The blue of this quilt is the peace and tranquillity
    Of Mother's disposition,
No sneer remarks or scolding words,
    Or unfair impositions.

Red is for Mother's love that warms me,
    Like love that Jesus brought to the world,
It melts the hate and stops the words
    That oft to others I might hurl.

Orange is kindness that Mother showed,
    Extended to all of mankind.
Kindness in return for unkind deeds
    Will always and always outshine.

Yellow is for joy and happiness,
    May we always and ever rejoice.
Though sorrows and trials come our way,
    We are comforted by Mother's voice.

Pink is a faith so firm and strong,
    Instilled by Mother from the start,
Faith in Christ and our fellowmen,
    Faith in ourselves to do our part.

Brown is the humbleness that Mother has,
　　To stoop to the lowliest task.
What is my pay or my reward?
　　Are questions she never asks.

Purple is her repentance,
　　To right an unintentional wrong,
To bring each one to harmony—
　　Dissensions cannot last long.

Grey are the tears she shed for me,
　　When I hurt or did some misdeed.
Tears that washed my broken spirit,
　　And calmed my every need.

White is for her forgiveness,
　　So exampled within our home.
We must forgive as we are forgiven,
　　No matter where we roam.

Young Mother: "The Weaver"
　　My life is but the weaving
　　Between my God and me
　　I only choose the colors
　　He weaveth steadily
　　Sometimes He weaveth sorrow
　　And I in foolish pride
　　Forget He sees the upper
　　And I the under side.

　　Not till the loom is silent
　　And the shuttles cease to fly
　　Shall God unroll the canvas
　　And explain the reason why
　　The dark threads are as useful
　　In the skillful Weaver's hand
　　As the threads of gold and silver
　　In the pattern He has planned.

Song: "More Like the Master"

Laborer of Love

Beth Guye Kittle

"Someday," she said, "I'll stop and rest.
I'll read good books and eat the best
Of all the food I always craved."
(The days flew past—and still she gave.)
"Sometime I'll shop for pretty clothes
And go to see the latest shows,
And hike for miles through the autumn's haze—
Or while away the winter days
Before a cozy fireplace
In silken gowns all trimmed with lace."
(The winters passed—and springs—and falls—
She scarcely knew they came at all.)

"Why, someday I shall have my hair
All waved and curled, and I shall wear
That good perfume I used to buy"—
(Was there a memory in her eye?)
She smiled and spoke of what she'd do
When all her work at last was through,
And there was time to live the way
She meant to do "some future day."

And so about her many tasks
She gaily went and never asked
For recompense, except to feel
Their gratitude and friendship steal
About her life, until at last
Her "somedays" in the busy past,
Had led her on to the greatest goal—
God's welcome smile and the home of the soul.

And so on earth she never knew
Those "someday" things she meant to do.
But all her labors born of love
The Lord remembered up above.
And even yet she bends her head
To tuck a cherub into bed—
And smiles to think how sweet to be
In God's "someday"—eternally.

CHILDREN'S DAY

Children of the World

E. Gano Karns

Participants: Four girls and four boys—dressed in native costumes. (As each child finishes speaking, he or she joins the others on the platform.) One teenaged girl to read query poems.

Preparation: The teenager is seated at a table or on a chair or couch reading a book on missionaries. As she finishes the book, she lays her head back and closes her eyes.

Exercise

Teenager: My, what a wonderful story—
How thrilling it must be
To be a missionary
In lands across the sea.

(She hears a door open, sits up, and sees a little girl dressed in Chinese costume come upon the stage. As the child walks up to her, the teenager speaks.)

Teenager: Little girl from China
Tell me, do you know
That Jesus died to save us
Because He loves us so?
China: I was once in darkness
For I was lost in sin
Until the missionary came
To tell me of his king.

(After speaking, she walks to the side of the stage.)

48

(Miss Japan enters and walks up to the teenager.)
Teenager: Pretty black-eyed beauty
        From faraway Japan,
        Do you know that Jesus
        Died for every man?
Japan: For many years my people
        Worshiped the emperor,
        Until the missionaries came
        To open Heaven's door.

(Miss India enters.)
Teenager: Little girl from India,
        Have you never heard
        The story of our Jesus
        From out of God's Holy Word?
India: My folks were very unlearned,
        They really didn't know,
        And so they worshiped many gods
        Among them the sacred cow.

(Boy from Philippines enters.)
Teenager: Little boy from the Philippines
        Tell me is it true
        That no one has ever told you
        That Jesus loves you, too?
Philippines: My people of the Philippines
        Followed false teachers, too,
        Until some real true Christians came
        To tell the story true.

(Boy from Mexico enters.)
Teenager: Little boy from Mexico,
        Land of bright sunshine,
        Did you know that Jesus died
        For your sins and mine?
Mexico: My people like some others
        Were led by ignorant men
        Who did not know the Savior,
        Or that He died for them.

(Boy from Germany enters.)

Teenager: Little boy from Germany,
          Land of Luther's fame,
          Have you heard the message
          Of why our Savior came?
Germany: Once my people were misled
          By men from ancient Rome,
          But reformation heroes led them
          To seek a better home.

(Miss Italy enters.)
Teenager: Little girl from Italy,
          Land across the sea,
          Do you know that Jesus
          Died for you and for me?
Italy: My people have for many years
          Followed where they were led.
          They worshiped many different things
          And many saints now dead.

(Miss America enters.)
Teenager: Little girl from America
          Home of the free and the brave,
          Do you know and have you told
          That Jesus came to save?
America: My land was once the home of
          The Indian wild and free
          And then the Pilgrim fathers came
          To worship as they pleased.

(As Miss America joins the others on the platform, the teenager joins them, too.)

Together: And yet in every country
          Many are still lost in sin,
          Won't you help in every way
          To carry the Word to them?

(At the close of the exercise, the audience could join the group on stage in singing "Send the Light.")

For Children's Day

Evelyn Witter

Prelude: "All Things Bright and Beautiful"

(Children enter church and advance slowly toward the front. Each child wears a pastel-colored, crepe-paper hat of floral design. The hats need not be elaborate to be effective, and they should resemble buds more than fully grown flowers.)

Setting: At the front of the church place four small vases and one large vase or flower basket.

There are four speaking parts and one verse for the entire group. The four children who have the speaking parts are in the center of the group. They stand and face the auditorium.

After each one of the four speaks his lines, he turns and places his flower in one of the smaller vases. Then he takes his place at the end of the line in order that he may act as a leader in seating the group when the exercise is over.

First Child: Flowers brighten Children's Day—
And make us happier along the way.
(Places flower in vase.)

Second Child: These flowers we have come to share.
They speak of God's kind, loving care.
(Flower in vase.)

Third Child: Flowers are the sign of spring,
And tell God's love for everything!
(Flower in vase.)

Fourth Child: Flowers are so sweet and mild,
Like whispered prayers of a small child.
(Flower in vase.)

(There is soft music as background for the prayer. Children bow their heads.)

Prayer: By teacher or superintendent

O Lord, Thou hast been the inspiration of our children. We open our hearts to Thee this Children's Day. We as parents trust in Thee, and our children love Thee. Help us all to remember God's love for us, that we may return that love in constant service. May our hearts ever be glad that we are all Thy children. Amen. (Pause.)

Children (in unison, holding flowers forward):

We, too, are buds that flower and grow
As the word of God points the way to go!

(The children follow their appointed leaders to their seats, placing their flowers in the big vase or basket as they go. The background music is "Jesus Loves Me!")

PROMOTION DAY

Garden of Promise

(Departmental Program)

Hazel Bacon

Properties: (Grass colored material may be used to cover the platform—gives an out-of-doors effect. Two or three firm boxes, or a footstool, covered with gray crepe paper, may look like rocks when placed at far end. Open Bible should be placed on a stand at side.

A ladder may be used in center. Each rung is labeled with a class name and shows growth through promotion. Start on the bottom rung with the Beginner Class and work up to the Adult Class.

These department names may be printed on white paper or cardboard in black ink or crayon. They can be attached to each rung with tape. Letters four or five inches high may be seen.

Cast: Knowledge (older teenage girl in cap and gown, with strong, pleasing voice—leadership ability). She stands near the ladder as names are called, in turn, by the one in charge of each group.

Class members. All those to be promoted will have their names called. Those with the speaking parts can be selected by the teachers of the classes represented.

Knowledge: I am Knowledge. I have learned through experience and studying—books. The most important book to me (motion to Bible on stand) is the Bible. Today is a special day at (name of church), God's house on God's earth. It is Promotion Day.

Promotion is very much like our ladder here. We begin (motion) way down here where it says (use name of youngest class on the ladder), then up, up, to the (last name of class on ladder).

Step by step we learn—first from our parents, then from our teachers and minister. I am still learning—many things.

We will find out, as names are called, if some of our children and young people deserve to be promoted. (Knowledge repeats each announced name as she welcomes them.)

Beginner: (Girl, aged 4, stands to one side until invited into the garden after speaking.)
I am a Beginner. I cannot remember all my lessons real good, but I do love Jesus very much. Am I promoted?

Knowledge: Yes, indeed, (mention her name), you are promoted. Welcome to the Garden of Promise through promotion. (Motion for her to sit on one of the pretend rocks.)

Next!

Beginners: (They stand at side after reciting until invited into the garden.)
(Girl) I have been in the Beginner's Class. I know that God made our world—and people. I know that God sent Jesus. Am I—promoted?
(Boy) I have learned what is right, and I—know what is wrong. I have been in the Beginners. Am I promoted?

Knowledge: Welcome to our garden, (use first names). You are both promoted to the Primary Class. (She motions them to stand back of girl sitting on rock.)

Next!

Primaries: (Enter girl and boy from Primary Department. Girl points to lower part of ladder.)
(Girl) I have been in the Beginner's Department and the Primary Department. I know many Bible stories, and I try to be helpful and kind. Am I promoted? (Boy) I have been in those classes, too. I have learned to listen. I come—almost every Sunday—and I love my Bible. Am I promoted?

Knowledge: (Call them by first names), we see our Bible—like a ladder—leading up and up. Yes, dear children, you are both promoted from the Primary Department to the Middler Department. (Motions them to stand back of one of the rocks.)

Are there others?

Middlers: (Girl) We are from the Middler classes.
It is good to be promoted,
And we like Promotion Day.
We keep right on using our Bibles—
We are pleasing God that way.
(Boy) When Jesus was teaching on this earth, He was often very tired. But He was never too tired to talk to the people about Him, because He loved them. We try to follow His example. Knowledge, are we promoted?

Knowledge: You are both ready for promotion to the Junior Department. Go stand in our Garden of Promise.

Next!

Juniors: (Girl) We are Juniors.
I have often been promoted,
And all of this I like to tell.
I have learned the Lord's Prayer—
And Bible stories I know quite well.
I'm glad God is—everywhere.
I'm glad I can learn—and grow.

55

I'll study to be a teacher,
Then more of the Bible I will know.

(Boy) Promotion to me is—like a ladder. Class by class we reach up. But—sometimes to me, it is like a drinking cup. "Come unto me," said Jesus, "and ye will never thirst." Knowledge, are we worthy of promotion?

Knowledge: You will, indeed, be promoted, both of you. Promoted from Junior to Junior High. Go—join the group in the garden.

Any others?

Junior High: (Girl) We are from the Junior High Class.
We are wealthy, indeed, to know our Lord,
As we study our Bibles, so true,
It is good to hold on to the gems we find,
For they guide us, our whole life through.

(Boy) Our Bible is like a ladder, leading us up and up!
We listen, and learn from God's Holy Word.
We drink in His wise demands.
If we climb, and fall, we don't give up.
We know He loves us well.
We reach out, and He holds us close,
Until we are safe—again.

Knowledge: Junior Highs, with God's blessing, you are promoted to the High School Department.

(Welcomes High School girl and boy by first names. They study ladder while speaking.)

High School: (Girl) Knowledge, I have been a Senior. I guess I belong in the adult group, if I deserve it. I am older now, but Bible study tells us age makes no difference with God. We are all His children—all still learning. May we all be active in Bible work, have more humility, and witness in honor of God.

Knowledge: (To boy) And you?

> (Boy) If promoted, I will keep up my religious studies. I pray that I may overcome too much love of self, and that God will make me strong. I will continue to serve Him well.

Knowledge: I am proud of you both. You are promoted from Senior High to Adult classes. May God give you wisdom and be with you always.

(Now would be a good time to call the names of all those being promoted in each class if you have not done so already.)

Knowledge: (Motions to the others.) Come, we will all sing one verse of "Trust and Obey." (Some other appropriate song can be used, but if a second verse is sung, invite the audience to join in.)

Promotion Day

(Exercise for Juniors)

E. Gano Karns

P   rogress is the milestone, that we reach each day
On our way to Heaven—promotion is the way.

R   ighteous folks should see that we must really strive,
If we love our Savior, and walk by His side.

O   nward, ever striving for that heavenly goal—
Praying, studying, learning, building up our soul.

M   ore like Christ our Savior we would ever be,
So each year we study, very faithfully.

O   nly as we serve Him here upon this earth,
Just so we shall see Him, and have His new birth.

T   rying every Lord's Day, in our Bible school,
To be more like Jesus, and live by His rule.

I   n all ways we hope to please God's Son, The Word,
That we might grow up as folks who love our Lord.

O   thers we must strive to Christ our Savior bring,
That they might accept Him as their Lord and King.

N   ever, if we falter on the upward way,
Will we see our Savior up in Heaven one day.

D   uty's not the only thing that we must do.
If we love our Savior, we must serve Him, too.

A   nswer as He calls us to obey His will,
Live and love and serve Him, and our need fulfill.

Y   ou must now obey Him, as we all must do,
This all spells Promotion Day—you must seek it, too.

FATHER'S DAY

Faith's Beginning

(A Modern Day Play)

Faith Shaw

Characters: Miss Nelson, teacher of teenage class
Bob, teenager
Teenagers

Scene: As scene opens, a Bible-school class of teenage people has just been dismissed. The teacher is standing beside her desk while the class is leaving by ones, twos, or threes, chatting as they pass through the door. Chairs are disarranged and papers are scattered. The last one leaves.

Miss Nelson: Whew! I'm glad that's over! Where do they get their pep? (Hums to herself as she straightens the room.) They are such a fine group of young people. I shouldn't get so impatient with them. But when Susie and Jill began exchanging snapshots right in the middle of a serious discussion . . . and when Joe tilted his chair back, I really shouldn't have spoken so sharply . . . but he might have fallen. (Clasps hands and looks upward.) Oh, Father, give me patience and understanding!
(As she continues to pick up papers, a timid knock comes at the door. It opens slightly and Bob looks in.)

Bob: Miss Nelson?

Miss Nelson: Yes, Bob? Can I help you?

Bob: Are you too busy to talk to me? I could come back later.

Miss Nelson: No, of course I'm not too busy! Come right in. We'll sit over here (motions to two chairs) while we talk. O.K.? (They sit down. Miss Nelson waits as Bob hesitates.) What is it, Bob? I'm here to help, you know.

Bob: Miss Nelson, I've got to talk to someone. But I'm almost ashamed to . . . to . . . mention it. I just don't know what to do!

Miss Nelson: Well now, Bob, suppose you tell me all about it. Maybe when it's out in the open it won't seem so bad. Surely we can find the right solution with God's help.

Bob: That's just it! It's about God. (Pauses.) Miss Nelson, you know my Dad. Is he a Christian?

Miss Nelson (startled): Why, yes! I'd say he was one of the finest Christians in our church. Why, Bob?

Bob (blurting out): Then why, when we kids have such a good Christian dad and mother, can't I accept what's told me? Why do I have to know the reasons for some of their beliefs? I know the things they tell me are true . . . and then I read an article or hear some of the fellows talking, and I begin to wonder if the Bible is just a history book, like they say it is. Why can't I have the complete faith in it that Dad and Mom have? I'm ashamed of my doubts, but what can I do? (He rests his head on his hand.)

Miss Nelson: Why don't you talk to your dad about this, Bob? He could advise you much better than I.

Bob (looking up quickly): Oh, no! I couldn't tell Dad. He'd never be able to understand how his son could feel this way! You mustn't mention it to him, ever!

Miss Nelson: Of course I won't mention it to him, if you don't want me to, but somehow I think he'd understand. You see, Bob, everyone has faced doubts at some time in his life. It's what we do about them that counts. If a person is never faced with a doubt or a question, it probably means that that person isn't thinking or growing in his faith. Asking questions and securing answers to honest doubts is a way of learning. It strengthens one's faith rather than lessens it. But, Bob, do you remember the Scripture verse about faith that you learned years ago?

Bob (quoting): "Faith is the substance of things hoped for, the evidence of things not seen."

Miss Nelson: Yes, the "evidence of things not seen." You know, Bob, your little brother, Scott, doesn't demand proof that your dad and mother are who they say they are; he just accepts their love and care and loves them in return. It's this childlike faith God wants of us. (Pauses for a moment.) When John the Baptist was in prison (you remember, he was the one God sent to tell the world of the coming of the Savior), he also had his doubts and sent his messengers to ask Jesus if He really were the Messiah. Do you recall Jesus' answer? (Bob shakes his head.) He didn't say, in so many words, "Yes, I'm the Messiah." Instead He told John, by the messengers, to think of all the things he had heard that Jesus was doing—healing the sick, giving sight and hearing, restoring life—and then he'd know. Jesus didn't hold John's doubts against him, and neither will He hold your doubts against you, Bob. But He did suggest that John think over the things he knew concerning Him. Perhaps God has an important work for you Bob—a work that requires a strong confidence in Him, a clear and definite faith—and has stirred up your mind so that you must struggle with these questions and doubts. In this way you may acquire a surer faith, a more unshakable belief in Him whom we haven't seen, yet know exists.

(They sit quietly for a few moments.)

Miss Nelson: Shall we ask God now to increase our faith and to help us find the answers to the questions that plague us?

Keeping a Promise

(A Play for Teenagers)

Christine E. Scott

Characters: Bob Wilson
Judy Wilson
Dan Carter
Susie Carter

Time: Early afternoon, the day before Father's Day. Bob Wilson is busy at a small table. There is a pile of business letters and papers and some cardboard folders beside him. Another chair is at one side.

Bob: (Looking up as if at a clock.) It's nearly time to go to the Saturday game and I still have all this work to do! (Gives big sigh!) I'll never make it!

(Enter Judy, his sister. She is carrying a brightly wrapped package.)

Bob: What's that, Sis?

Judy: My present to Dad for Father's Day tomorrow. It's a lamp for his desk.

Bob: That's nice. I saw Dad looking at a great set of tools in the hardware store. He'd like that, and I'd sure like to get them for him.

Judy: I know he would.

Bob: But with my *very* flat billfold, all I could afford was a tie.

Judy: Well, I just hope it isn't awful looking.

Bob: 'Course it isn't. Wish I could get that set of tools, though!

Judy: It's almost time to leave for the game. (Looks out the window.) Dan and Susie are coming right now!

Bob: But I have to finish this filing for Dad before I can go. It's real important . . . And I promised.

Judy: Well, hurry! (Puts down package and goes to door.) Come on in! We're about ready.

(Enter Dan and Susie Carter.)

Bob (pointing at letters): Quite a bunch to do yet. You'd better start without me.

Dan (coming to back of table): What do you have to do?

62

Bob: These letters and papers have to be in the folders in alphabetical order.

Dan: You've been helping your Dad in his office a lot lately, haven't you?

Bob: Two weeks now. And Dad promised to pay me ten dollars today. *Ten dollars!*

Susie: Can't you do it after the game? (She sits in chair at one side.)

Bob: Wish I could, but Dad needs this done tonight.

Dan: Ask him if you can do it later.

Bob: He's not here. He had to go to Grover City on business. Won't be back 'til about seven tonight. And he'll need this right then. And I promised.

Judy: And Dad always says everyone should keep a promise.

Bob: He sure does!

Dan: But if he isn't even here—how can he keep *his* promise to you about the ten dollars *today?*

Bob: He had to be in Grover City in a hurry. I can wait. (Bob turns back to his work.)

Susie: Oh, Judy, are you ready for what we're doing in our Sunday-school class tomorrow for Father's Day?

Judy: You mean each of us telling about one of the men in the Bible? I'm going to tell about Abraham, the father of Isaac.

Dan: I'm choosing the father that forgave the prodigal son in that story that Jesus told.

Susie: I'm going to read about Jacob—the father of Joseph. He must have been a good father.

Bob: Fathers are pretty great today, too!

Dan: Right! My Dad taught me a lot about riding my bike. But he made me learn all the safety rules first. Guess that shows he really cares.

Susie: He spends a lot of time with us, too. Sometimes just talking about things.

Dan: You see? *Dads* are great! So, come on, Bob! Do this work later. Your Dad won't mind!

Bob (slowly): I really want to. But still—I promised. And Dad says—

Susie: Well, we'd better go! (Rises.)

Judy: Maybe you'll be done before the game is over.

Bob: I'm going to finish, anyway. I *did* promise.

Dan: We'll see you later at the game!

(Judy, Dan, and Susie hurry off. Bob works a few minutes, putting the papers into the folders, talking to himself: "Johnson goes under J-o . . . Brown—under B-r . . . etc.")

Bob: There! I'm done! (Gets up, stretches.) I've missed most of the game, but I feel just great! I'm glad Dad made me see it's important to keep a promise.

(Glances down at table. There is a large white envelope on it.)
What's this big envelope? It must have been under that last letter. (Picks it up.) It has my name on it! What— (Opens envelope quickly and reads.)
Dear Bob:
Here is the ten dollars I promised you today. I knew I could count on you to finish this. Thanks, Son.

> Love,
> Your Dad

(There is a pause. Then he holds up a ten-dollar-bill.)
Say! I'll just have enough time to get to the hardware store for that set of tools!
(Faces congregation.)
Thanks for *everything,* Dad!

Looking Up to Daddy

It might be just because I'm small
  my Daddy looks so very tall—
But I believe he'll always be
  the biggest man in the world—to me!

B. J. Hoff